# MAKING
# BIRTHDAY CARDS

MAKING

# BIRTHDAY
# CARDS

24 easy projects for a special birthday greeting

Consultant Editor: Stephanie Weightman

NEW
HOLLAND

Published in 2005 by
New Holland Publishers (UK) Ltd
London • Cape Town • Sydney • Auckland

Garfield House
86–88 Edgware Road
London W2 2EA
United Kingdom
www.newhollandpublishers.com

80 McKenzie Street
Cape Town 8001
South Africa

14 Aquatic Drive
Frenchs Forest, NSW 2086
Australia

218 Lake Road
Northcote, Auckland
New Zealand

ISBN 1 84330 906 8

Editor: Gareth Jones
Editorial Direction: Rosemary Wilkinson
Photographer: Shona Wood
Design: Axis Design Editions Ltd
Template Illustrations: Stephen Dew
Production: Hazel Kirkman

1 3 5 7 9 10 8 6 4 2

Reproduction by Pica Digital PTE Ltd, Singapore
Printed and bound by Times Offset (M) Sdn Bhd, Malaysia

**Note**
The author and publishers have made every effort to ensure that all instructions
given in this book are safe and accurate, but they cannot accept liability for any
resulting injury or loss or damage to either property or person, whether direct
or consequential and howsoever arising.

**Acknowledgements**
Special thanks to Fiskars UK Ltd (Newlands Avenue, Bridgend, Wales CF31 2XA) for
supplying equipment for use in this book.

# CONTENTS

Birthdays are some of the most special occasions we celebrate each year and to receive a hand-made card increases the excitement with that added personal touch. With this in mind you will find something for everyone in this book. There are 24 inspirational cards commissioned from a range of renowned card making designers. The designs are fresh and funky, traditional and elegant, and fun and humorous... You are guaranteed to find something suitable for the lucky recipient.

The beauty of making birthday cards is that when you make and give someone a hand-crafted card, you are telling them how special they are to you. Hand-crafted birthday cards stay on display longer than any shop-brought greeting and are admired by everyone who sees them.

If you have ever been tempted to make your own birthday cards now is your chance... Stop trawling those card shops, get out your crafting things and make that special, personal greeting that will be received on the day with delight and cherished for years to come.

Stephanie Weightman

# GETTING STARTED

This chapter describes the tools and techniques used to make the cards in this book. Check that you have all the things you need before you begin. Once you have mastered a few of the projects, you may want to be creative and adapt them, using the materials and paper you have, as well as the exciting odds and ends you will find once you start looking! Keep a special "card" box and, as you discover things, store them there, so that you have all your treasures in one place.

Paper and craft shops will stock most of the things you need. The basic tools and equipment are listed in this section, but be sure to check the list of materials needed for each card before you begin.

## PAPER & CARD

**PAPER AND CARDBOARD:** When buying paper and card the abbreviations "mic" and "gsm" refer to various thicknesses and weights of the papers and cardboards. The abbreviation "mic" is used when describing thickness and is short for microns, i.e. 1000 microns equals 1mm. The abbreviation "gsm" is used when describing the weight and is short for grams per square metre, i.e. a piece of 100 gsm paper measuring 1m$^2$ weighs 100 grams. A good weight to use is 230–260 gsm as this will be easy to fold and, at the same time, will not be too flimsy.

**SUGAR PAPER:** This paper is thick, with a slight texture, and is very reasonably priced. Because it is relatively cheap, it is a good paper to practise on, but you will need to use a double layer if you want it to be a card base.

**HANDMADE PAPERS:** Handmade papers are widely available in good stationery shops, artists' supply and crafts shops. There is a huge variety of colours and textures available, and you can also choose between paper with inclusions or without, and

translucent or opaque paper. Of course you can also make your own handmade paper.

**TISSUE PAPER:** This paper comes in a range of colours, and is good to print or stencil on but is too flimsy to be used as a card blank, unless backed with something more substantial.

**OTHER PAPERS:** Holographic card, metallic-effect paper and card, pearlescent paper, textured and corrugated card, and a range of all kinds of other materials can be obtained from general and specialist stationery shops and artists' suppliers. Glitter-effect papers sometimes have a self-adhesive backing. Some high-street chains also offer pre-packaged selections of funky papers and card.

**PAPER SIZES:** Standard sizes used in this book are A4 (210 x 297mm/8¼ x 11¹¹/₁₆in) and A5 (148 x 210mm/5¹³/₁₆ x 8¼in). A5, folded in half, gives you the standard size greetings card to fit a C6 envelope. Sheets of paper and card can be bought in larger sizes (A1 or A2) from specialist paper suppliers and cut to suit your requirements.

# PENS, PENCILS & PAINTS

**FELT TIPS, MARKERS AND GEL PENS:**
These are available in every colour you can think of, and a range of tip sizes. They are useful for everything from marking borders to writing messages.

**SILVER AND GOLD MARKER PENS:**
Metallic colours look great on both light and dark backgrounds.

**PENCILS:** Pencils must be kept sharp for accurate marking. An HB pencil is a good hard pencil for marking edges to be cut – use a softer pencil, such as a 2B, if you think you are going to make mistakes and need to rub the line out. A good eraser is also important for this reason.

**PAINT:** A selection of watercolour and acrylic paints is also useful. Metallic acrylic colours come in a variety of shades – choose the more glittery ones for best effect. Always use good quality paint brushes – they will not leave hairs on the paper after painting.

# CUTTING & SCORING EQUIPMENT

**CUTTING MAT:** If you use cardboard for cutting on, it retains score marks from a craft knife or scalpel, so it will need to be changed frequently. Using a cutting mat is much easier as it self-seals so your craft knife will not get stuck in previous score marks. The cutting mat allows the blade to sink into the material while cutting through the paper or card.

**CRAFT KNIFE:** A good, sharp craft knife is essential to keep your cut edges neat, so you may need to change your blade frequently. This also eliminates torn edges resulting from cutting paper with a blunt knife. Most craft knives come with blades which you can snap off when they become blunt. Scalpels can also be used – these are very sharp, so be very careful and have a supply of spare blades to hand if you are going to be doing a lot of cutting. *It is very important to take great care when cutting – never cut towards your body. Have plasters handy just in case!*

**SCISSORS:** Do not use scissors reserved for cutting fabric on paper or card as the paper will blunt the blades. It is handy to have a couple of different sizes of scissors – a large pair for general work and a small pair, like nail scissors, for fiddly detail. Pattern-edge scissors can create amazing effects. Be careful when lining up the pattern from cut to cut. A pair of scissors with a smaller pattern can be used for details and a larger pattern for more dramatic results.

**RULERS:** A metal ruler is a good edge to cut against. If you haven't got a metal ruler, it will be worth investing in one, as the blade on a craft knife can cut into the surface of a plastic ruler and ruin your work. A paper guillotine is also useful, but not essential, as is a set square, to help you cut accurate right angles.

## ADHESIVES

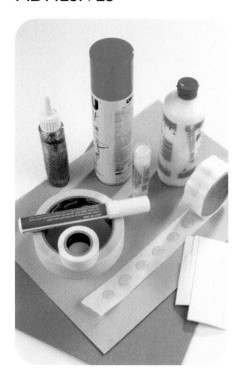

You will need a range of different glues when card-making, including:

**PVA ADHESIVE:** This is a strong water-based glue which forms a permanent bond when used on paper and board. It dries leaving a transparent finish.

**GLUE STICKS:** You can buy glue sticks with a fine tip which can be useful for writing. Glitter or embossing powder can be sprinkled over the glue.

**GLITTER GLUE:** This also comes in different thicknesses and many different colours. A fine tip applicator makes it easy to write out greetings.

**SPRAY ADHESIVE:** This is commonly used for sticking paper to paper or board as it has the great virtue of sticking firmly. Repositioning can be possible for up to 30 seconds after bonding two surfaces. Always protect the area surrounding the paper or object you are spraying with newspaper. Spraying into a box is a good way of

protecting surfaces. Remember to use in a well-ventilated room and carefully read the instructions on the can!

**ALL-PURPOSE CLEAR ADHESIVE:** This is a strong, cement-like adhesive used for sticking objects together. It is ideal for mixed media and fabric and dries leaving a transparent finish.

**STICKY TAPE:** Cellophane tape, masking tape, doubled-sided tape, magic tape, glue dots and foam pads are all useful. Sticky foam pads can be used as an alternative to glue when you are working with the more lightweight craft materials. Masking tape can be useful when spraying glue on specific areas of a card or blocking out certain colours when colouring. Sticky foam pads can be used as an adhesive and also create a 3D effect.

**COCKTAIL STICKS/COTTON BUDS:** These are very handy for applying glue to small or fiddly items.

## OTHER STUFF

**STAMPS:** Stamps can be bought in all shapes and sizes from shops or by mail order from specialist stamp manufacturers. Ink-pads come in all the colours of the rainbow as well as in gold, silver and bronze. Special embossing ink-pads can be used in conjunction with embossing powder to create a raised effect when the embossing powder is heated to melting point. When using stamps for decoration, make sure they are evenly covered with stamping ink.

**PUNCHES:** these come in a range of shapes and patterns, and are used to make delicate cut-out motifs in paper and card. The punched-out bits can also be used for decoration the front of the cards or on gift tags and envelopes.

**TWEEZERS:** Use tweezers to pick up and move smaller items such as quilled elements, or confetti.

**RIBBLERS:** Ribblers are a great little piece of equipment used to create corrugated card or paper. Plain paper is passed through the ridged rollers, whilst turning the handle on the side. The paper passes out of the back of the ribbler and can then be cut to size.

**GLITTER AND CONFETTI:** Glitter and confetti is available in a range of shapes and colours and is available from many card and stationery shops. It can be used on cards or simply loose in the envelope as a surprise.

**COLLECTIBLES:** Lace, shells, coins, old photographs and postcards, stamps, buttons, ribbons, raffia, feathers and much more can be found in flea markets, haberdashery shops or even your home. Keep all of these things in labelled envelopes, where necessary, to make life easier for yourself. Similarly, make up a file for magazine cuttings, wrapping paper and pieces of handmade paper.

**PRESSED FLOWERS:** At least two weeks in advance of making your card, press all the flowers, leaves and petals you wish to use in a heavy book between sheets of blotting paper or smooth tissue paper and leave to dry in a warm, dark and dry place. To avoid mould use less succulent flowers.

# CARD MAKING TECHNIQUES

**CUTTING AND SCORING:** You will need a craft knife, steel ruler and cutting mat to score or cut medium-weight cardboard or thick paper. First, take the card and cut it to the desired size using a set square and ruler to make sure the corners are square. On the outside of the cardboard, measure the centre line where the card will fold and mark it with a pencil. Make sure the pencil mark is parallel to the edge, or the card will not fold properly. Then, using the metal ruler and craft knife, lightly score over the pencil line but make sure only to score the top layer of the cardboard with your craft knife.

**CUTTING A WINDOW:** Use a ruler to measure the centre of the front of the card and mark lightly with a pencil. Then, using a set square, mark out where you wish to have the window, using the centre mark as a guide. Check the window is centred correctly by using a ruler to measure from the edge of the card to the edge of the window. With the card opened flat on a cutting mat, carefully cut out the window using a ruler and sharp craft knife. Move the card around when cutting each edge so you are always cutting parallel to (never towards) your body. Cut with the window on the inside of the ruler so you can see where the pencil lines begin and end. Take care not to extend the cuts beyond the corners of the window.

**TORN EDGES:** An attractive finish to your card or the design within your card is a torn edge, which is a characteristic of many handmade and water-colour papers. To achieve this effect, measure and mark with a pencil where you wish the torn edge to be. Fold the paper over along this line so that you have a crease to work with. Firmly hold down the ruler against the crease and tear the paper by pulling away or towards you. Do a little at a time and press the ruler down firmly to avoid ripping the paper where you don't want it to tear.

# MAKING ENVELOPES

Although most of the projects in this book are a suitable size for envelopes of the common sizes you will find in most stationery shops, it can often be more appropriate to create a matching envelope for a handmade card. Making an envelope is a fairly easy task and the advantage of a handmade envelope is that it will colour co-ordinate perfectly with your card. Follow the instructions on this page to make an envelope.

## you will need

- sheet of paper approximately three times the width of your card
- scissors
- pencil
- metal ruler
- glue stick

1 Place the greetings card centrally on the bottom edge of the sheet of paper. Fold the sheet of paper down over the greetings card. Open up the sheet of paper.

2 Place the card along the fold line you have just created. Fold the paper up over the greetings card (it should cover the card). Next, fold the paper down over the greetings card.

3 Open up both folds. Now fold the side sections of paper inwards over the card. Open up the two new folds. You should now have four fold lines.

4 Place the sheet of paper onto a cutting board, and using a craft knife and metal ruler, cut away the four rectangular sections marked by the fold lines in each corner of the sheet of paper. You should be left with two large flaps on either side of the central section. These flaps will become your tabs.

5 Use the pencil to mark up 1cm (½in) wide tabs on each flap. Use the craft knife to trim away the excess paper.

6 Fold the lower section of the card upwards and use a glue stick to stick the tabs down over what will form the back of the envelope. When you have placed the greetings card in the envelope, fold the upper back of the envelope down over the card and use a glue stick to seal your envelope.

**PACKING AND PADDING:** Each week a huge number of cards travel through the post and via courier companies. Often the outside packaging gets damaged, so it is important to ensure that the more delicate your card is, the more protection you give it. Nothing is more heartbreaking than to make and send a beautiful card only to find it was damaged by the time it got to its destination. Gift-wrap your creation with tissue paper or cellophane to make it extra special, then send in a padded or stiff-backed envelope.

**DECORATING ENVELOPES:** You can personalize envelopes in lots of ways: make one yourself from beautiful textured, handmade paper; wax-seal your envelopes; wrap the finished card and envelope in contrasting tissue or crepe paper and tie with gold cord; or embellish your envelope flap with small decorative elements from the card inside.

**GIFT TAGS:** If you have left-over card, fabric, paper or other material from making a card, why not create a matching gift tag? You can also adapt elements of many of the projects in this book to a much smaller format and use them as gift tags.

Here is an overview of all the birthday cards in this book. I am sure there is something to spark your interest. All that is left to do is to choose the card you want to make first.

Pretty in Pink p.16

Coloured Foil Flower Pot p.18

Bouquet of Tulips p.20

Make a Wish p.22

Flower Power p.24

Beaded Parcel p.26

Die Cuts With a Difference p.28

Good Enough to Eat! p.30

Foil Letter p.32

Romantic Red Rose p.34

Coluzzle Daisies p.36

Quilled Flower p.38

Trio of Roses p.40

Lavender Blue p.42

Pretty as a Picture p.44

Flickering Flame p.46

Little Black Cat p.49

Finger Puppet Clown p.52

Man at Work p.54

Handbag Delight p.56

Tic Tac Toe p.58

21st Celebrations p.61

Aquarium Shaker p.64

Pop-up Parrots p.66

# PRETTY IN PINK

Using pretty pink translucent paper over rose pink card with silver gel pen decoration, this birthday greeting is incredibly simple and quick to make. You might want to draw different shaped balloons more appropriate to the greeting, for example circles or stars.

## you will need

- A5 sheet of pink card
- cutting mat
- soft pencil and metal ruler
- set square
- craft knife
- eraser
- pink translucent paper
- glue stick
- silver gel pen

## tip

Using the card design you can make elegant gift tags. Tie them with ribbon to pink tissue paper-wrapped presents.

**1** Measure a rectangle 10 x 21cm (4 x 8¼in) on the pink card. Cut out the rectangle and fold it in half. This will be your basic card. Measure and cut a piece of pink translucent paper to the same size. Fold in half, then open up. Erase any remaining pencil marks.

**2** Measure and mark out a window 5.5cm (2¼in) square in the centre of the front of the translucent paper.

**3** Using the craft knife, carefully cut out the window in the translucent paper. Take the square you have cut out and keep it on one side. Erase any remaining pencil marks.

**4** Run the glue stick down the spine of the pink card and fix it inside the folded translucent paper. Then use the silver gel pen to draw swirl shapes and a freehand silver border around the cut-out square.

**5** Using the 'window' of translucent paper you removed earlier, cut out a 3cm (1¼in) square shape. Attach it centrally using the glue stick. Use the silver gel pen to draw on three heart-shaped balloons and a border.

# COLOURED FOIL FLOWERPOT

A pot of flowers is a perfect gift, and the one on the front of this card is no exception. The metallic flowers add more than a little extra sparkle to complete that special someone's day.

## you will need

- A4 sheet of blue foil card
- A4 sheet of white card
- cutting mat
- soft pencil and metal ruler
- craft knife
- eraser
- A5 cream card
- ribbler
- Coloured Foil Flower Pot template (page 69)
- glue dots
- scissors
- scrap of green foil card
- sequin die cuts (1 square, 3 flowers, 3 sun-shapes, 3 leaves)
- glue stick

## tip

Ribblers reduce the length of the card, so play it safe and always use more card than you think you will need.

**1** Taking the blue foil card, mark out a rectangle 5 x 9.5cm (2 x 3¾in) and cut it out with the craft knife and ruler. Taking the white card, measure a rectangle 20 x 21cm (8 x 8¼in) and cut out, then measure halfway along the short side, score and fold.

**2** Taking the cream card, cut a strip approximately 8.5cm (3⅜in) wide. Using the ribbler, ribble the strip, then cut off a 4.5cm- (1¾in)-long section. Using glue dots, stick the ribbled card to the centre of the blue foil rectangle.

**3** Using the template, transfer the pot shape onto the reverse of the blue foil card. Cut the shape out and, using the glue dots, fix the pot to the ribbled card, allowing room for flowers on top. Cut a strip from the green foil card 0.5 x 2cm (¼ x ¾in) for the stem. Tuck the stem behind the flowerpot. Fix the pot to the ribbled card allowing space for the flowers on top.

**4** Take your ready-made green foil leaves and, using glue dots, fix them to the rim of the pot. Then, again using glue dots, fix the three flowers to the ribbled card, one above the other, above the leaves and on the stem.

**5** Pick up the sun shape and, to add further dimension, squeeze gently between your fingers to create a scrunched effect.

# BOUQUET OF TULIPS

Perfect for a birthday, this exquisite and colourful paper and wire collage card shows the time and care taken to make it and will convey your love and friendship to the happy recipient.

## you will need

- A4 sheet of white cartridge paper
- A4 sheet of white handmade paper
- metal ruler
- all-purpose glue
- 4 lengths of raffia, 25cm (9¾in)
- scissors
- 2 pieces of yellow handmade paper, 5 x 8cm (2 x 3⅛in)
- 10cm (4in) square piece of white organza
- Bouquet of Tulips template (page 69)
- pencils in pink, blue, yellow, purple, orange and green
- 0.4mm- (⅛in)-diameter gold jewellery wire
- pliers
- 20cm (8in) length of blue ribbon
- 20cm (8in) length of small pearls
- small leaves from the garden
- A5 sheet of yellow card folded in half

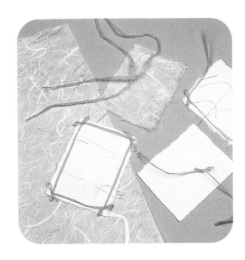

**1** Measure and tear two 7 x 9cm (2¾ x 3½in) rectangles – one each from the cartridge paper and the white handmade paper, and glue together. Take two raffia lengths and tie a bow near the centre of each. Glue the bows to the inside edge of the handmade paper at opposite corners. Trim the lengths to fit and glue. Make two more bows from the remaining raffia and glue these in the other corners.

**2** Take the first piece of yellow paper and cut the corners off to form a kite shape. From the second piece, cut a triangular shape to fit the bottom of the kite shape, and carefully glue in place. For extra decoration, cut an organza triangle slightly larger than the triangle. Place over the bottom of the kite shape, then fold and glue down the overlap on the back of the kite shape.

**3** Copy 14 tulip heads and stalks onto the cartridge paper, from the template. Colour in six pink, two blue, two yellow, two purple and two orange heads with the pencils. Colour the tulip stalks green. Cut out the tulips. Make 4–5 golden swirls from the jewellery wire with the pliers and tie a blue bow out of the ribbon. Cut one length of two pearls and one length of three pearls.

**4** Glue the kite shape onto the white rectangle made in step 1. Glue the flowers inside the pocket of the kite and add individual pearls, leaves and wire swirls. Glue the ribbon bow and the two lengths of pearls at the bottom of the bouquet and decorate with a single pink flower and two of the small leaves from the garden, then glue the collage on to the front of the yellow card blank.

**5** For extra decoration on the back of the card, tear a 3.5 x 4.5cm (1⅜ x 1¾in) rectangle out of the cartridge paper and white handmade paper and glue together. Glue one pink tulip and two leaves to the centre and decorate the edge with raffia as before. Glue to the back of the card.

# MAKE A WISH

At first glance this looks like a glass-painted card, but in fact felt markers and outline stickers create the look. Simply apply the outline stickers to acetate and colour in the gaps with the marker pens. Keep it simple – three or four colours create a striking effect.

## you will need

- A4 sheet of white card
- cutting mat
- soft pencil and metal ruler
- craft knife
- eraser
- A5 sheet of yellow card
- A5 sheet of acetate
- happy birthday cake outline sticker
- permanent marker pens in a selection of colours
- glue stick

## tip

By using the tip of a craft knife (or a pricking tool) to pick up your outline sticker you can hold it over your card and check the position before sticking it in place.

**1** Taking the A4 white card, measure and cut out a 12 x 24cm (4¾ x 9½in) rectangle. Measure halfway along the long side, then score and fold. Measure and cut out a window 7cm (2¾in) square inside the front of the card.

**2** Taking the yellow card, measure and cut out a 9cm (3½in) square. Then measure and cut a window 7cm (2¾in) square in the centre of the card. Finally, taking the acetate, measure and cut out an 8cm (3⅛in) square.

**3** Carefully remove the outline sticker from the backing sheet and hold it over the acetate to check the position. Once you are happy that it will fit and the borders look good, place the outline sticker in position. Gently rub over the design with your fingers to make sure it is stuck down.

**4** To colour in the outline sticker on acetate you should use permanent marker pens. They are transparent when dry, giving the look of glass paints, but do not smudge. Keep the colours to a maximum of three or four and do not go outside the the edges of the stickers. Leave the acetate to dry for a short while.

**5** Once the acetate is dry, position it in the window so that the birthday sticker is in the centre of the card. Use a glue stick or glue dots to hold the acetate in place. Finally position the back frame inside the card so the edges of the two windows match, and glue it in place.

# FLOWER POWER

Bright and cheerful is the best way to describe this card. Fresh, colourful daisies sit simply in the centre of the purple window frame. You could use pastel colours for a softer look.

## you will need

- A5 sheet of white card
- cutting mat
- soft pencil and metal ruler
- craft knife
- eraser
- A5 sheet of light purple paper
- glue stick
- Flower Power (flower, leaf, pot) templates (page 69)
- scraps of dark blue, red, yellow, orange and lime green paper
- glue dots or glue stick

## tip

For a realistic look, cut each of the flowers out twice and use 3D foam pads to mount them on top of each other.

**1** Taking the A5 white card, measure halfway along the long side. Score and fold the card in half, and erase any left-over pencil marks.

**2** Taking the light purple paper, measure and cut out a rectangle 10 x 12.5cm (4 x 5in). Then mark out a window 6.5 x 9cm (2½ x 3½in) in the centre of the purple paper. Cut out the window and glue it in position on the front of the card approximately 1cm (⅜in) down from the top edge.

**3** Using the pot template, copy the design onto the scrap of dark blue paper and cut it out. Take a craft knife and, working on the cutting mat, create extra detail with a line of small horizontal cuts between the rim and base of the pot.

**4** Using the flower template, transfer the design onto the reverse of the red, yellow and orange paper scraps, and cut out each flower. Using the leaf template, copy the design twice onto the reverse of the lime green paper and cut out the two leaves.

**5** Using the glue dots or a glue stick, position and attach the flowerpot so that it sits on the bottom edge of the window. Place the flowers onto the card, making sure you are happy with their position, then glue them in place. Fix the leaves so they peep out from behind the flowers.

# BEADED PARCEL

This pretty centre-opening card is perfect for a girlfriend or relation. Wire and beadwork is
enjoying a revival and, after seeing how simple and effective this card is, is it any wonder why?

## you will need

- A4 sheet of white card
- cutting mat
- soft pencil and metal ruler
- craft knife
- eraser
- A5 sheet of dark pink mottled paper
- A4 sheet of mottled pink card
- glue stick
- Beaded Parcel (bow, knot) templates (page 69)
- scissors
- extra fine gold wire
- 25–30 seed beads – a mixture of clear and coloured (e.g. red, purple)
- glue dots

## tip

To change the look of the card, replace the cut-out bow with one made from ribbon.

**1** Taking the white card, measure, and cut out a rectangle 12 x 17cm (4¾ x 6¾in). Measure 6cm (2⅜in) in from the left, along the long side, score and fold. Taking the remaining piece of white card, cut out a 7cm (2¾in) square. Then cut out a 6.5cm (2½in) square from the dark pink mottled paper and stick it to the centre of the white square. Erase any pencil marks.

**2** Taking the pink mottled card, measure and cut out two rectangles 7 x 12cm (2¾ x 4¾in) in size. Glue the first to the outside of the white card flush with the edge of the left-hand flap, the second to the inside of the white card, flush with the right-hand edge.

**3** Take the the left-over piece of white card, and, using the bow template, transfer the bow-shape on to it. Do the same for the knot, then measure a rectangle 3 x 4cm (1¼ x 1½in) for the parcel. Cut out the shapes with the scissors.

**4** Take a length of wire and secure one end to the back of the parcel using a glue dot. Begin to wind the wire around the parcel, threading beads as you work. Once you are happy with the number of beads you have threaded and the amount of wire you have used, secure the loose end to the back of the card using another glue dot.

**5** Position the parcel and parcel bow in the middle of the dark pink square. Glue the left-hand half of the square to the front flap, so that the square and the parcel sit centrally when the the card is closed.

# DIECUTSWITHADIFFERENCE

If you need to make a quick and easy greeting, this card is just for you. Simple yet effective, the jazzy flowers couldn't be easier to punch and assemble. Try alternating the colours between pastels and brights for an entirely different look.

## you will need

- 2 x A4 sheets of cream card
- cutting mat
- soft pencil and metal ruler
- craft knife
- eraser
- A5 sheet of red paper
- A5 sheet of yellow paper
- A5 sheet of silver card
- medium-sized daisy punch
- 3 paper fasteners
- A5 sheet of acetate
- glue stick

## tip

This design works very well with any flower punch. Vary the size of the window to suit the size of flowers. Use sequins and glue to imitate paper fasteners if they are unavailable.

**1** Taking the first piece of cream card, measure and cut out a 21cm (8¼in) square, then score and fold in half. Open the card and mark out three windows 5.5cm (2¼in) square, spacing them evenly down the front of the card at approximately 1cm (⅜in) intervals, and cut them out with the craft knife. Erase any pencil marks that are left.

**2** To make the daisies, take the sheets of red and yellow paper and, using the daisy punch, punch three daisy shapes in each colour. Place the red daisy to the bottom with yellow on top, slightly twisted so the red petals are visible underneath. Use a craft knife to make a small hole in the centre of each and push the paper fasteners through.

**3** Measure and cut out three 4.5cm (1¾in) squares from the red paper, three 4cm (1½in) squares from the cream card and three 3.5cm (1⅜in) squares from the silver card. Glue the layers together to form three square mounts. Taking the three daisies, push each paper fastener through the centre of each square, and fold back the legs of the fastener to hold the daisies in place.

**4** Taking the acetate, measure and cut a rectangle 8 x 20cm (3⅛ x 8in). Place the acetate inside the front of the card behind the three windows so that no edges are visible and mark on the corners of each window. Glue the daisy squares onto the acetate in the centre of each window, and fix the acetate in place on the inside of the front of the card.

**5** Taking the second piece of cream card, measure and cut out a rectangle 10 x 20cm (4 x 8in), and fold in half along its length. This will be an insert to disguise the back of the acetate. Glue the insert to the inside back of the card, with the fold line flush with the card's fold line.

# GOODENOUGHTOEAT!

This easy-to-make cup-cake card makes a really mouth-watering greeting,
with an added glitter topping for that extra birthday sparkle.

## you will need

- A4 sheet of shiny purple card
- cutting mat
- soft pencil and metal ruler
- craft knife
- eraser
- scrap of red holographic card
- Good Enough to Eat! (cherry, icing, cake) templates (page 70)
- scrap of white card
- A5 sheet of cream card
- scissors
- PVA adhesive
- A5 sheet of white parchment
- pink glitter
- glue stick

## tip

Decorate the icing with a sprinkling of small, columned bugle beads to look like "hundreds and thousands".

**1** Taking the purple card, measure a rectangle 11 x 22cm (4⅜ x 8¾in), and cut out. Fold in half along the long edge, and score. Erase any remaining pencil marks.

**2** Take the red holographic card and copy the cherry template onto the reverse, copy the icing template onto the piece of white card, and the cake template onto the cream card. Cut out the shapes with the scissors.

**3** Take the PVA adhesive and apply it generously to the top of the icing-shape. While the glue is still wet sprinkle on the pink glitter. Tap off any excess and leave to dry. Then, with the glue stick, glue the cherry to the top of the cake and the icing over the cherry so its top edge lines up with the top edge of the cake shape.

**4** Taking the sheet of parchment paper, measure and cut out a rectangle 5 x 13cm (2 x 5⅛in). Place the parchment onto the work surface and pleat it along the length, with pleats approximately 0.5cm (¼in) wide. Erase any remaining pencil marks.

**5** Position the cream card with icing onto the centre of the card and glue it in place. Fold the edges of the bun case in, then place the bun case over the cake so that the cake looks as if it is inside the case. Finally, glue each of the sides in position.

Using peel-off stickers can give stunning effects, especially when used with holographic card. The 3D effect was created by using foam squares. Easy to achieve but very striking!

## you will need

- A4 sheet of white card
- cutting mat
- soft pencil and metal ruler
- craft knife
- eraser
- A5 sheet of blue mirror card
- tweezers
- A5 sheet of gold holographic card
- gold peel-off sticker sheet (envelope and hearts design)
- scissors
- glue dots
- 3D foam pads

## tip

It can be difficult to pick up small stickers with fingers. Use a pair of tweezers or the tip of a craft knife to help pick them up and position them onto your card.

**1** Taking the white card, mark out a rectangle 15 x 21cm (6 x 8¼in), then score and fold halfway along the length. Erase any pencil marks.

**2** Taking the blue mirror card, measure a rectangle 4 x 12cm (1½ x 4¾in) and cut it out. Taking the gold holographic card, measure and cut out a rectangle 3.5 x 10cm (1⅜ x 4in). Glue the gold rectangle to the middle of the blue rectangle, then place glue dots on the back of each corner of the blue card and mount it onto the front of the card.

**3** With tweezers, pull the heart peel-off from the backing sheet and mount onto a left-over piece of blue mirror card, then cut a small square border around the heart. Taking the scrap of white card, cut out a rectangle 3 x 6cm (1¼ x 2⅜in) and fold in half along the long edge. Mount the mirror heart onto the mini-card with glue dots.

**4** Use the tweezers to remove the envelope and hearts peel-off from the backing sheet. Mount the peel-off onto the remaining blue mirror card. Using the scissors carefully cut around out the outline of the peel-off, taking particular care when cutting out the hearts.

**5** Apply small 3D foam squares to the back of both the mini card and the blue envelope. Peel the backing off the 3D foam squares and mount the card and envelope onto the holographic gold to complete the card.

# ROMANTIC RED ROSE

This is the perfect birthday card for a loved one, combining layers of handmade paper and a single pressed rose, to get them in the mood for a romantic celebration.

## you will need

- A3 sheet of white handmade paper
- soft pencil and metal ruler
- set square
- scissors or craft knife
- eraser
- A4 sheet of pink handmade paper
- glue stick
- A5 sheet of cream textured card
- pressed rose
- gold marker pen

## tip

Choose flowers that aren't too 'fleshy' as they may go mouldy in the press.

**1** Measure and cut out a rectangle 22 x 26cm (8¾ x 10¼in) from white handmade paper. Fold it in half, then in half again to make a double layer card base. Erase any pencil marks.

**2** Next, measure and cut out a rectangle 8.5 x 10.5cm (3⅜ x 4¼in) from the pink handmade paper. Erase any remaining pencil marks. Use a glue stick to attach it in a central position on the card base.

**3** Measure and cut out a rectangle 6 x 9cm (2⅜ x 3½in) from the cream textured card. Erase any pencil marks. Glue the rectangle centrally on the pink handmade paper rectangle.

**4** Use the glue stick to attach the pressed rose to the card. Make sure you handle the rose carefully, as it will be very delicate.

**5** Using a ruler and the marker pen, draw a gold border on the white handmade paper around the edge of the card and on the cream card around the rose.

# COLUZZLE DAISIES

This project is based around the technique of coluzzle – a larger and more detailed form of lacé, perfect for anyone wanting a little more of a challenge. To undertake something this intricate you must have a sharp craft knife.

## you will need

- 14 x 28cm (5½ x 11in) piece of white card
- cutting mat
- soft pencil and metal ruler
- craft knife
- large daisy coluzzle template
- magic tape
- scissors
- A4 sheet of red paper
- eraser
- glue stick
- 3D foam pads
- Coluzzle Daisies template (page 70)
- corner daisy punch
- back felt pen

## tip

For other coluzzle templates, choose a punch design that complements the overall shape of the card.

**1** Taking the piece of white card, measure and score halfway along the long edge. Using the coluzzle template as a guide, draw a daisy shape on to the front of the card, ensuring you overlap the folded edge slightly. Cut out the daisy shape with the scissors through both layers.

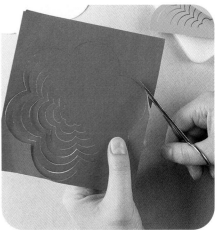

**2** Take the red paper and, using the card blank as a template, transfer the daisy shape onto the paper. Then place the coluzzle template inside one half of the daisy shape, and tape down. Using the craft knife, cut through the lines of the template. Then cut around the daisy shape outline using the scissors.

**3** Align the edge of the red daisy-shape with the edge of the white card and glue the solid half in place. Working from the inside out glue down the central daisy, then carefully fold the next petal strip over. Then repeat the process of alternate glued-down and folded strips until you reach the outside edge. This will create the daisy pattern.

**4** Carefully position 3D foam pads onto the red side of the folded red petals and remove the paper backing. Stick the folded petals down.

**5** Taking the left-over white card, copy the template, cut it out, and glue it into the centre of the central red daisy. Using the corner punch, punch out six sets of small daisies and glue them to the outer edge of the large flower. Using the black fine felt pen, dot the centre of the daisies.

# QUILLED FLOWER

This intricate quilled flower card makes a lovely spring birthday greeting. The traditional craft of paper lace can be used to create stunning, delicate patterns and motifs. This project is perfect for nimble fingers.

## you will need

- 9 x 18cm (3½ x 7in) piece of yellow card
- 9 x 18 cm (3½ x 7in) piece of blue card
- cutting mat
- soft pencil and metal ruler
- craft knife
- eraser
- PVA glue
- quilling tool or round pencil
- white, orange and yellow quilling paper
- cocktail stick or matchstick
- tweezers

## tip

If you want to send the card in the post, use a padded envelope or cushion the flower design with a piece of bubble wrap. If you present the card in person, you might want to embellish the envelope with a tiny quilled flower on the flap.

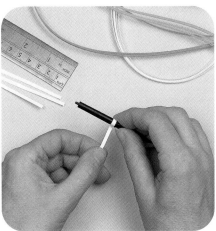

**1** Take the two pieces of card, and measure halfway along the long edge of each, score and fold. On the front of the yellow card, cut out a square window 2cm (¾in) in from the edges. Take the blue card and trim 3mm (⅛in) off all open sides. Apply a thin line of glue along the fold line of the blue card and stick it down just to the right of the fold line inside the yellow card.

**2** To make the petals, tightly wind a 15cm (6in) strip of white quilling paper around the middle of the quilling tool. Ease off and leave the quilling paper to unwind to the desired size.

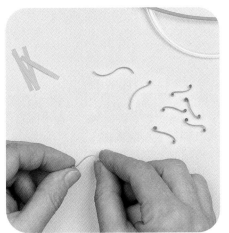

**3** Pinch one end of the loose coil to make a teardrop-shaped petal. Fix down the loose end of the strip with a dab of glue – use a cocktail stick or matchstick for this. Make another five petals in this way.

**4** Make the orange curls by bending the ends of a 3cm (1¼in) strip of quilling paper in opposite directions using you fingernail, then roll tiny curls between thumb and forefinger. Finally, make the centre of the flower out of a 1cm (⅜in) strip of yellow quilling paper, rolled tightly between thumb and finger. Glue down the loose end.

**5** Starting with the centre coil, pick up each quilled element with the tweezers, dab spots of glue on the underside using the cocktail stick and position on the blue background within the yellow frame. Next, position the orange curls at even intervals, radiating out from the centre. Finally, stick down the white petals.

# TRIO OF ROSES

Pre-embossed images are perfect to use when time is of the essence and a professional finish is required. Using pre-embossed roses, this beautiful but simple-to-make birthday greeting truly says it with flowers.

## you will need

- A5 sheet of light pink card
- cutting mat
- soft pencil and metal ruler
- craft knife
- eraser
- deckle-edge scissors
- A5 sheet of dark pink paper
- A5 sheet of light pink paper
- glue stick or PVA glue
- line cutter (optional)
- No Stamp Required modern rose (pre-stamped and embossed image)
- small paintbrush and water
- pink and green metallic paint
- 3D gloss
- length of pink ribbon
- superglue or other strong glue

## tip

Try using 3D gloss over gel pens, felt-tip pens or even glitter to give an ultra-high shine to coloured detail.

**1** Take the light pink card, score and fold in half. Using the deckle-edge scissors cut a 3mm (⅛in) strip from the long edge of the front of the card. Cut a strip from the dark pink paper 15cm (6in) long and 2cm (¾in) wide. Glue this to the inside of the card butted up to the long edge and trim to fit.

**2** Use the line cutter (or a craft knife and metal ruler) to cut out two pink squares – a dark pink square approximately 7.5cm (3in) square and a light pink square approximately 7cm (2¾in) square. Glue the light pink square to the centre of the dark pink square.

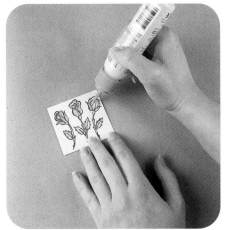

**3** Take the sheet of pre-embossed roses and cut out a 6.5cm (2½in) square containing three roses. Check that they fit inside the small pink square. Colour the flowers and the petals with the pink and green metallic paint, diluting with water to fade the colour.

**4** Coat the flowers and leaves with a thin layer of 3D gloss to highlight them. Leave the sheet on a flat surface and allow the gloss to dry for a few hours.

**5** Glue the pink squares to the front of the card, then glue the roses centrally on top of the squares. Tie the ribbon into a pretty bow and cut a V-shape into the ribbon ends. Fix to the card with the superglue or other strong glue.

# LAVENDER BLUE

This card could carry a message of love to someone special on their birthday. It would be particularly meaningful if the lavender was from your own garden. You will need to pick and press the lavender during the summer months.

## you will need

- A4 sheet of lavender blue paper
- cutting mat
- soft pencil and metal ruler
- craft knife
- set square
- A5 sheet of white textured card
- eraser
- glue stick
- 3 stems pressed lavender flowers
- scissors
- PVA glue
- paint brush
- pressed heart-shaped seed heads
- silver paint

### tip

Instead of silver hearts you could use small stars or silver swirls to embellish the card.

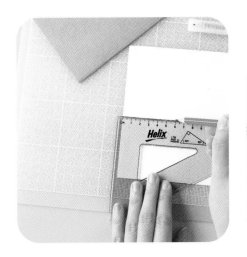

**1** Taking the lavender blue paper, measure halfway along the long edge, score and fold. Use the set square and pencil to measure a rectangle 6 x 9cm (2⅜ x 3½in) onto the white textured card, and then cut it out. Erase any pencil marks that remain.

**2** Using the glue stick, apply glue to the back of the white card rectangle and attach it to the card base in a high central position.

**3** If necessary, trim the lavender stems. It is best to keep the stem that will be used in the centre of the card slightly longer than the other two. Coat the back of each stem with PVA glue and position on the card.

**4** I was fortunate to find some heart-shaped seed heads in the garden which I pressed and painted silver. If you can't find anything like this, you might want to cut some small heart shapes from a piece of silver card. Use PVA glue to attach the silver heart shapes to the card.

### extras

Use can adapt the design to make simple but beautiful gift tags.

These quilled daisies almost pop out of the picture at you. This card is perfect for a loved one and guaranteed to brighten anyone's day. It will also allow you to indulge in one of the most relaxing crafts there is.

## you will need

- A4 sheet of white card
- cutting mat
- soft pencil and metal ruler
- craft knife
- Pretty As A Picture template (page 69)
- A4 sheet of purple paper
- glue stick
- eraser
- 5mm and 10mm quilling papers in cream, purple, pink, lilac and pale yellow
- quilling tool
- spring clip
- decoupage or nail scissors
- A5 sheet of green paper for the leaves and stems

## tip

This beautiful 3D card looks delightful framed as a picture for the wall.

**1** Taking the piece of white card, measure and cut out a 21cm (8¼in) square, then score and fold in half. Using the template, copy the vase on to the purple paper and carefully cut it out. With the glue stick, fix the vase to the middle of the card towards the bottom. Erase any remaining pencil marks.

**2** Take a strip of cream paper and place the end in the quilling tool. Wind the paper round the tool to make the flower centre. When the centre is approximately 0.5cm (¼in) in diameter, tear off the excess and glue in place. Repeat for each flower, making some in yellow and lilac as well.

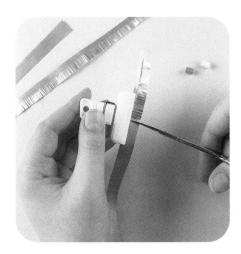

**3** Take a strip of purple, pink or lilac quilling paper and use the spring clip to hold the paper. Snip small cuts, using the scissors along the full length of paper strip.

**4** Take one of the cream flower centres and apply a small amount of glue to the edge. Start to wind the frilled paper around the centre, winding until the the flower petals look full. Repeat to make six small flowers, five medium flowers and three large flowers (or as required), in a mixture of colours.

**5** Arrange each of the flowers, smallest at the top then glue them in position using a glue stick or glue dots. Taking the green paper, cut thin strips approximately 5cm (2in) long, for the stems, and oval shapes in varying sizes, for the leaves. Tuck the stems and leaves amongst the flowers. Fix them in position with the glue stick.

# FLICKERING**FLAME**

Once you have completed your first iris-folding card you will soon discover the simplicity of this fabulous technique and want to move on to something a little more advanced. This candle card is perfect for celebrating a special occasion.

## you will need

- A4 sheet of cream card
- cutting mat
- soft pencil and metal ruler
- craft knife and scissors
- Flickering Flame (iris-fold, window) templates (page 70)
- eraser
- adhesive tape
- A4 sheets of patterned paper in two different designs
- A4 sheets of plain paper in gold and red
- glue-stick
- red felt-tip pen
- A5 sheet of cream card

## tip

If tracing the iris-fold pattern you will need to work from the back of the tracing or reverse copy it.

**1** Take the A4 sheet of cream card. Score halfway along its length and fold it in half.

**2** Transfer the candle-shape template on to the front half of the cream card.

**3** Carefully cut out the candle-shape to form the window. Erase any remaining pencil marks from the card.

**4** Cut out the iris-fold template leaving a wide border of paper around it. Fully secure it to the table with adhesive tape, taking care not to tape over any of the numbers. With the card face down, align the window to the iris pattern. Secure with tape.

**5** Cut the pattern and plain paper into strips that are approximately 2 x 12cm (¾ x 4¾in).

**6** Fold all of the cut-out strips in half along their short sides, right side out.

**7** Place the first piece of patterned paper, folded edge towards the centre over box no.1, and secure with adhesive tape. Next take the gold paper and fix this over box no.2, the red paper over box no.3 and the other patterned paper over box no.4. This is the base of the iris-fold pattern.

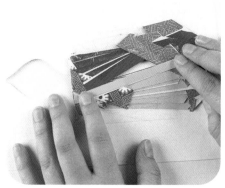

**8** As you stick down the papers in ascending numerical order, you must ensure that the four colours and patterns are the same from each of the four edges to the centre.

**9** Take the red paper and cut out a rectangle of sufficient size to cover the flame area of the window. Secure it with adhesive tape.

**10** Cut a smaller flame shape from the gold paper and glue it to the middle of the large flame. With the red pen, mark a smaller flame shape in the middle of the gold flame.

**11** Take the A5 sheet of cream card and, using the gluestick, secure the card over the back of the iris design to hide the rough, taped-down edges.

# LITTLEBLACKCAT

A great card for cat lovers... Sitting by the window, watching the goldfish and the world go by,
a cute little black cat is wondering who will come out to play.

## you will need

- A4 sheet of white card
- cutting mat
- soft pencil and metal ruler
- craft knife and scissors
- eraser
- watercolour paints
- paint brush and water
- silver peel-off strips
- A4 sheet of red paper
- A4 sheet of purple paper
- Little Black Cat (fish, cat, bowl) templates (page 71)
- A4 sheet of silver card
- A4 sheet of acetate
- A4 sheet of orange foam
- A4 sheet of black card

## tip

As an alternative design, leave the goldfish out of the bowl and use silk flowers, to create the 3D effect of a flower-filled vase.

**I** Taking the piece of white card, measure and cut out a rectangle 12 x 24cm (4¾ x 9½in). Measure and mark halfway along the long edge, score and fold. Erase any pencil marks.

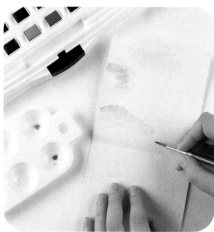

**2** With the watercolour paints, on the inside back of the card, create a colour wash to represent the sky and a small amount of greenery. This will be the window area.

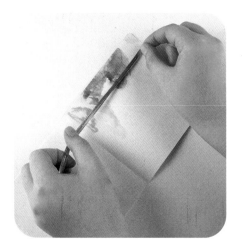

**3** To make the window frame take two strips of silver peel-offs from the backing. Arrange them in a cross-shape, with the vertical strip 2.5cm (1in) from the left-hand edge of the inside back and the horizontal strip approximately 4.5cm (1¾in) from the top edge of the inside back, using the picture as a guide.

**4** To make the curtain, take the piece of red paper and cut out a 12cm (4¾in) square. Pleat this piece of paper in 2cm (¾in) pleats, fixing the pleats in place with the glue stick at the top edge. Then glue the curtain on to inside back of the card from the right-hand edge of the card to approximately half-way across.

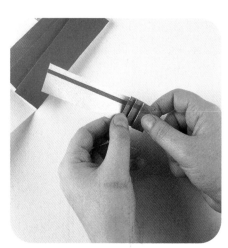

**5** Taking the purple paper, cut a strip 2cm x 18cm (¾ x 7in). Next, cut a thin strip of the red paper 3mm (⅛in) wide. With the glue stick, carefully fix the strip across the purple paper near the top edge. Pleat the purple paper in 2cm (¾in) pleats, fixing them in place with the glue stick at the top edge, and then glue the purple strip along the top of the card.

**6** Using the bowl template, transfer the shape onto the back of the sliver card, and cut the bowl out. Repeat on the sheet of acetate, cutting the acetate slightly longer at the top and bottom.

**7** Take the orange foam and, using the fish template, transfer the shape onto it, and carefully cut out with the scissors.

**8** Now glue the foam fish to the centre of the silver fish bowl shape.

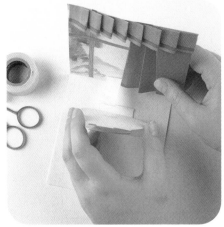

**9** Position the acetate bowl-shape over the silver bowl-shape, so that it bows out slightly. Use a small strip of silver peel-off to join the top edges of the shapes together. Fold the bottom edges of the shapes under and glue to the card.

**10** Taking the left-over white card, measure and cut a strip 1 x 5cm (⅜ x 2in) Crease and fold the card halfway along the long edge, and then 1cm (⅜in) from each end to form two tabs. With the centre fold pointing at the window, glue one tab to the inside base of the card and the other to back of the goldfish bowl. This will allow the card to stand open.

**11** Now using the little black cat template, copy the shape onto the black card, and cut it out. Bend the cat's tail at 90° to the main body. Using a glue dot, fix the cat's tail to the card in front of and to the right of the goldfish bowl, so that the cat sits upright.

# FINGER PUPPET CLOWN

Is it a card or is it a toy? A fun idea to send to the little ones in the family, this card can be made using whatever colours and materials you can conjure up from your box of collected bits and pieces.

## you will need

- A4 sheet of pink or flesh-coloured plain card
- felt-tip pen
- Finger Puppet Clown template (page 72)
- scissors
- A4 sheet of white card
- sheets of funky foam in red, purple and white
- all-purpose glue
- black marker pen
- orange felt-tip pen
- scrap of fake fur, matching the colour of funky foam (optional)

## tip

This finger puppet design not only makes a fabulous birthday card but also sets the theme for any children's birthday party. You can use the design for party invitations as well as birthday cards.

**1** Take the flesh-coloured card and on the back, using the felt-tip pen and the template, carefully copy the outline of the clown-shape. Cut it out with the scissors. Repeat for the white card.

**2** On the white clown-shape, with the felt-tip, draw in the shorts and fingerholes, the hat, top, ruffle, belt, cuffs and hatband, and cut each of the shapes out. Ensuring you have each one the right way up, use them as templates, and mark the shapes on to the desired coloured sheet of funky foam. Cut out the foam shapes.

**5** Using the flesh-coloured clown shape as a base, glue the funky foam shapes in the relevant places. Once all the shapes are glued in place, draw around each section with the black marker pen to give the clown a more cartoon-like appearance.

**6** Carefully cut the fingerholes into the shorts. If you want to add fun fur, make the holes slightly bigger than your fingers. Spread a line of glue around each of the holes, stick down the strips of fun fur and trim as necessary.

**7** Cut out four small circles from the red funky foam and a mouth shape from the white. Glue these in position, using two of the red circles for buttons, one for the hat and one for the nose. Draw around the edges of the buttons with black permanent ink pen. Colour in the hair with the orange pen.

# MANATWORK

Isn't it always difficult to find ideas for cards for men? It can be a struggle to make something that is masculine yet still stylish... Try this one for size – perfect for Mr DIY!

## you will need

- 12 x 24cm (4¾ x 9½in) piece of white card
- cutting mat
- soft pencil and metal ruler
- craft knife
- 7cm (2¾in) square of white card
- 8.5cm (3⅜in) square of pale blue paper
- 9.5cm (3¾in) square of royal blue paper
- eraser
- Man at Work (saw-blade, saw-handle, hammer-head, hammer-handle) templates (page 71)
- scrap of brown card
- scrap of matt silver textured card
- scissors
- glue stick
- 0.5 x 6cm (¼ x 2⅜in) strip of cream paper for the tape measure
- fibre-tip pen
- blue eyelets
- eyelet punch setter

**1** Take the 12 x 24cm (4¾ x 9½in) piece of white card, then score and fold halfway along the length. Next glue the white square to the centre of the pale blue square, glue the pale blue square to the centre of the royal blue square, and finally glue the royal blue square to the centre of the front of the card.

**2** Using the templates, copy the tool handle shapes onto the brown card, and the saw-blade and hammer-head shapes on to the silver card. Cut the shapes out using the craft knife or scissors. (If you have a pair of pinking scissors you can use them to make the teeth on the saw blade.) Stick the tools together with the glue.

**3** Take the strip of cream paper, using the fibre-tip pen and the ruler, mark out measurements along one edge to make the tape measure. Roll around a pen handle and glue in place, leaving a small amount of the strip sticking out so that the tape looks like it's unravelling.

**4** With the card open, take the eyelet punch setter and punch a hole through the corners of the light blue square. Take a blue eyelet and push it through the hole from the bottom so that the tube piece is showing through. Using the eyelet punch setter, press down on the eyelet tube to hold the eyelet in place. Repeat in the other corners.

**5** Fix the tools and the tape measure in place with the glue. Use the pen to draw some nails and tacks beside the tools.

# HANDBAGDELIGHT

A new handbag is a must for any birthday. By using a variety of patterns and decorative card there are simply no limits to how many handbags a girl can have...

## you will need

- A4 sheet of bright pink pearl card
- cutting mat
- soft pencil and metal ruler
- craft knife
- eraser
- Handbag Delight (front flap, back flap, fastener) templates (page 73)
- A4 sheet of lilac pearl card
- glue stick
- gold scallop border peel-off
- scissors

## tip

This is a very versatile design. Decorate with sequins and gemstones to make an evening bag card – great for an 18th or 21st birthday.

**1** Taking the pink card, measure, and cut out a rectangle 10 x 20cm (4 x 8in). On the reverse, measure and mark along the long edges, top and bottom, at 8, 9, 10, 11 and 12cm (3⅛, 3½, 4, 4⅜ and 4¾in), and score. Fold towards you along the central fold and away from you along the first two and last two folds. Erase any pencil marks that are left.

**2** Transfer the front flap and back flap templates on to the back of the lilac pearl card and cut them out, taking care around the delicate butterfly shape on the front flap. Using a glue stick, stick the flaps to the front and back of the handbag, so that they line up.

**3** Using the fastener template, transfer the fastener shape onto the lilac pearl card and cut it out. Next, carefully cut out a slot for the fastener to fit through on the front flap (as marked on the template) and glue the fastener to the inside back near to the top of the card so that it fits snugly through the slot.

**4** Now using the gold peel-off, decorate the edges of the top flap of the handbag, paying particular attention to the butterfly shape. From the bottom of the gold peel-off cut two triangles of equal size and stick them to the bottom corners of the bag.

## variations

Use the back flap template on page 73 and patterned card for both sides of the handbag. Decorate the main section of the bag with punched-out butterflies from the coloured paper of your choice.

# TIC TAC TOE

A game of three-in-a-row played on this bright yellow gift card decorated with ladybirds and daisies should bring a smile to someone's face. A card and gift all in one!

## you will need

- A4 sheet of yellow card
- A4 sheet of white card
- cutting mat
- soft pencil and metal ruler
- craft knife
- eraser
- glue stick
- A5 sheet of green card
- Tic Tac Toe template (page 73)
- wavy-edged scissors
- 2 x 8cm (¾ x 3⅛in) piece of acetate
- piece of white card for the counters
- fine black pen
- orange and red felt tip pens
- scissors
- ladybird stamp
- black ink pad

**1** Cut the A4 sheet of yellow card in half. Fold one half in half along the long edge – this is the card base. Cut out a piece of white card 7cm (2¾in) square and a piece of yellow card 6.5cm (2½in) square. Glue the white square diagonally at the top of the card then stick the yellow square on top.

**2** Cut four narrow strips of green card, each approximately 7cm (2¾in) long. Using the photo for guidance, glue them across the square to create the game board.

**3** Trace and cut out the template. On the green card draw around the template and cut out the shape. Use wavy-edged scissors to decorate the outer edge. This is the pocket surround.

**4** Glue the pocket surround to the acetate and then glue the pocket to the bottom of the card. The pocket opening should face upwards.

**5** The counters are made from white card. Using the fine black pen, draw seven simple daisy shapes and decorate with orange felt tip pen.

**6** Carefully cut out the daisy shapes with the scissors, cutting just outside the black line.

**7** Use the ladybird stamp and the black ink pad to print five counters on the remaining piece of white card.

**8** Neatly colour in the ladybirds using the red felt tip pen. Cut them out carefully.

**9** Glue two of the daisies at the top corners of the card and place the rest in the pocket with the ladybirds.

## variations
Individual flowers and ladybirds make neat gift tags.

# 21st CELEBRATIONS

Start the celebrations in style with this fresh and funky card, perfect for a 21st birthday.
The floating champagne bubbles finish the card and complete the fizz, and, with this simple design,
the card can be altered for any age or celebration.

## you will need

- A4 sheet of white card
- cutting mat
- soft pencil and metal ruler
- craft knife and scissors
- eraser
- gold line peel-off border
- A5 sheet of white card
- 21st Celebrations (numbers, spray, bottle, cork) templates (pages 74–75)
- A5 sheet of gold card
- scissors
- scrap of red holographic card
- tweezers
- glue stick or PVA glue
- A5 sheet of acetate
- red holographic tape
- A4 sheet of blue paper
- thin gold wire
- adhesive tape

**1** Taking the A4 sheet of white card, score and fold in half along its length. On the inside of the card front, measure and cut out a window 9.5cm (3¾in) wide and 11cm (4⅜in) high, and 2cm (¾in) from the top and the sides. Erase any pencil marks that are left.

**2** Taking the gold peel-off border, remove a strip and frame the window leaving a small border (around 3mm (⅛in)), trimming as required with a pair of scissors or craft knife.

**3** Take the piece of A5 white card. Copy the measurements for the window in step 1 and cut it out. This piece of card will form the backing to hide where the wire is attached.

**4** Using the template for the bottle and cork, transfer the design on to the back of the gold card and cut the shapes out.

**5** Take the scrap of white card and cut out a 2.5cm (1in) square. Stick it to the front of bottle to the right. For the label, take the red holographic card, mark, measure and cut out a piece 1 x 2cm (⅜ x ¾in), then stick it to the white card. Finally, fix a small strip of holographic tape across the cork.

**6** Using the spray template, transfer the shape on to the acetate, cut it out, and glue it to the top and back of the bottle neck. Next, cut out circles from the red holographic tape, and fix them to the spray shape using the tweezers and the PVA glue.

**7** Using the templates for the 2 and the 1, transfer two pairs of shapes onto the blue paper – one pair in reverse. Cut four pieces of wire 5cm (2in) long. Secure the wire pieces to the top and bottom of the back half of the numbers and tape them down. Glue the front and back halves of the numbers together with the wire between them.

**8** Open the card, face down, and move the numbers into position. Use tape to secure the wires in place, then check how the numbers look from the front of the card.

**9** Take the bottle and position it to the bottom left of the window and slightly at an angle. Glue in place. Repeat with the cork but this time in the top right-hand corner as though it has popped from the bottle.

**10** Using the red holographic tape, cut out four small red bubbles. Using the tweezers, position them on the edge of the card below the cork, as required.

## variations

Using the alternative templates on pages 74–75, you can turn the card into a greeting for an 18th or a 40th birthday celebration. Change the colours to suit the personality, age and gender of the recipient.

# AQUARIUMSHAKER

Will the cat catch the fish or only get the bones? Shake this exciting card designed for cat (or fish) lovers and see the holographic fish sparkle in the light. A great card for children, too...

## you will need

- stamp ink pad
- stamp for frame design, approximately 10 x 14.5cm (4 x 5¾in)
- A4 sheet of white paper
- spray adhesive
- A4 piece of poly-board
- cutting mat
- metal ruler
- craft knife
- fish stickers or fish confetti
- A4 sheet of coloured card
- sharp nail scissors
- A5 sheet of white card, folded in half
- 2 x A5 sheets of acetate
- A5 sheet of aqua-coloured tracing paper or greeny-blue, slightly translucent paper
- Aquarium Shaker template (page 76)
- all-purpose glue
- cat stamp for inside of card

**1** Ink the frame stamp and stamp firmly onto the first sheet of white paper. Leave to dry, then apply spray adhesive and stick onto a piece of polyboard. Using the steel ruler and the craft knife, trim the polyboard close to the outside of the stamped design and cut out the centre to create a window.

**2** If you are using small fish stickers, peel them off the backing sheet and stick them onto coloured card. Cut them out with the scissors. You could also use nail scissors for this.

**3** Position the frame on the greetings card blank along the fold line and mark the outline and the inside window with a pencil. Trim the card to size and cut out the window from the front of the card using ruler and craft knife. Put to one side.

**4** Apply spray adhesive to the front of the frame and firmly press on to one piece of acetate, trimming the excess from the edge of the frame. Place the frame face down and position the fish, picture-side down, inside the frame. Using the template, cut out some seaweed shapes from the coloured tracing paper, spray one side with glue and stick them onto the second piece of acetate.

**5** Apply all-purpose glue to the back of the frame and position onto the seaweed-decorated acetate, creating a clear pocket with the fish inside. Trim off any excess around the frame. Glue the frame in position exactly over the window of the greetings card blank. Stamp the cat inside the card, so that it appears to look through the fish tank.

# POP-UP **PARROTS**

Pop-up cards can be quite difficult to make, but this one featuring bright and jolly parrots on a jungle background uses a simple movement.

## you will need

- A4 sheets of card in dark olive green, red, lime green and apple green
- cutting mat
- soft pencil and metal ruler
- craft knife
- eraser
- 2 x A4 sheets of sky blue translucent paper
- glue stick
- Pop-up Parrots (flower, foliage, parrots, stand) templates (pages 76–77)
- spray adhesive
- A4 sheet of white paper
- tracing paper
- scissors
- yellow gel pen
- paintbrush and water
- watercolour paints in yellow, dark and pale green, blue and red
- black marker pen

**1** Take the dark olive green card and cut a rectangle 12 x 24cm (4¾ x 9½in), then score and fold in half. Cut a 10cm (4in) square from the red card and glue it to the front of the card. Cut a 9cm (3½in) square of blue translucent paper. Using spray adhesive, back this with a square of white paper and glue to the red card with the glue stick.

**2** Using the pencil, transfer the stand template onto the other sheet of sky blue translucent paper. Apply spray adhesive and attach it to the sheet of white paper and cut along the pencil outlines and cutting lines for the pop-up. Fold in half, with the white paper on the outside.

**3** Fold back the first narrow tab and the large outer tab, then flatten down and open up the card.

**4** Now pinch and pull these tabs outwards to create the structure of the pop-up. Apply glue stick to the areas of the white paper that will stick on the card base and glue inside the green card.

**5** Using the foliage 1 and foliage 2 templates, copy both shapes onto the lime and apple green card and cut them out. Copy the flower template onto the red card and cut out the shapes.

**6** Using the glue stick, glue the various items in place inside the card. If any items overhang the sides, simply trim them.

**7** Now attach the branch and flowers to the front of the card. Highlight the red flowers used on both the inside and outside of the card with yellow gel pen.

**8** Trace the parrot template and draw four pairs of parrots. Paint the parrots, copying the colours in the photo above.

**9** Highlight and outline the parrots with black marker pen and add the eyes. Carefully cut out the parrots just outside the black outline.

**10** Stick three pairs of parrots in position on the inside of the card, on the tabs. Make sure you position them so that the card can close without creasing the parrots.

**11** Finally, using the glue stick, stick the fourth set of parrots in position on the front of the card.

# TEMPLATES

All the templates shown here are actual size. They may be easily enlarged or reduced on a photocopier if you wish to adapt a design to make a larger or smaller card. Dotted lines indicate fold lines.

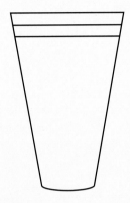

Coloured Foil Flower Pot/
Pretty As A Picture
(page 18/page 44)

Flower Power
(flower, leaf, pot)
(page 24)

Bouquet of Tulips
(page 20)

Beaded Parcel
(bow, knot)
(page 26)

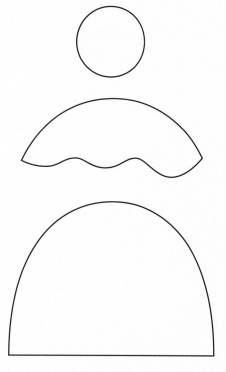

Coluzzle Daisies
(page 36)

Good Enough to Eat!
(cherry, icing, cake)
(page 30)

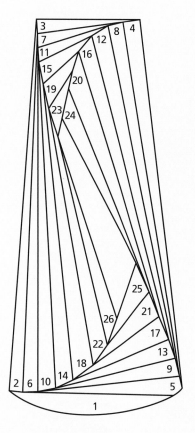

Flickering Flame
(iris-fold, window)
(page 46)

Little Black Cat (fish, cat, bowl)
(page 49)

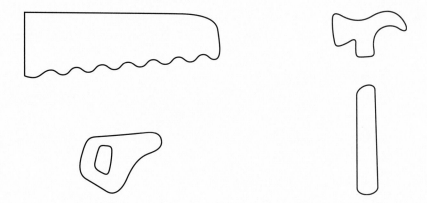

Man at Work
(saw-blade, saw-handle, hammer-
head and hammer-handle)
(page 54)

Finger Puppet Clown
(page 52)

Handbag Delight
(front flap, back flap, fastener)
(page 56)

Tic Tac Toe
(page 58)

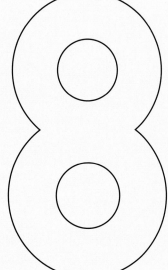

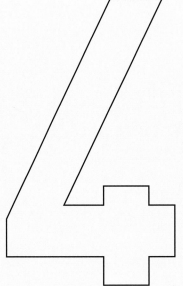

21st Celebrations
(numbers (for 18th & 40th also),
spray, bottle and cork)
(page 61)

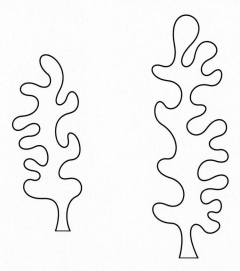

Aquarium Shaker
(page 64)

Pop-up Parrots
(flower, foliage 1,
parrots, foliage 2,
stand) (Page 66)

Fold forwards

Fold backwards

# SUPPLIERS

## United Kingdom

**Art and Crafts Direct**
Unit 44, Coney Green Business Park
Wingfield View
Claycross
Derbyshire
S45 9JW
Tel: 01246 252 313
www.artandcraftsdirect.com
*General craft supplier and mail order*
*supplier of No Stamp Required.*

**Blade Rubber Stamps Ltd.**
12 Bury Place
London WC1A 2JL
Tel: 020 7831 4123
Email: info@bladerubberstamps.co.uk
www.bladerubberstamps.co.uk
*Suppliers of stamps, border punches,*
*embossing powders, etc.*

**Cowling & Wilcox**
26–28 Broadwick Street
London W1F 8HX
Tel: 020 7734 9557
Email: art@cowlingandwilcox.com
www.cowlingandwilcox.com
*General craft supplier.*

**Craft Creations**
Ingersoll House
Delamare Road
Cheshunt
Hertfordshire
EN8 9ND
Tel: 01992 781 900
Email: enquiries@craftcreations.com
www.craftcreations.com
*General craft supplier.*

**Cranberry Card Company**
Unit 4, Greenway Workshops
Bedwas House Industrial Estate
Bedwas, Caerphilly
CF83 8DW
Tel: 02920 807 941
Email: info@cranberrycards.co.uk
www.cranberrycards.co.uk
*Selection of card, paper and accessories.*

**Creative Crafts**
11 The Square
Winchester
Hampshire SO23 9ES
Tel: 01962 856266
Email: sales@creativecrafts.co.uk
www.creativecrafts.co.uk
*General craft supplier.*

**The English Stamp Company**
Worth Matravers, Dorset
BH19 3JP
Tel: 01929 439 117
Email: sales@englishstamp.com
www.englishstamp.com
*Suppliers of stamps, paints, inkpads and*
*handmade paper. Mail-order only.*

**Falkiner Fine Papers Ltd.**
76 Southampton Row
London WC1B 4AR
Tel: 020 7831 1151
*Carries a large range of handmade papers.*
*Also offers a mail-order service.*

**Fiskars Brands UK Ltd.**
Brackla Industrial Estate
Bridgend
Mid Glamorgan CF31 2XA
01656 655 595
Email: anthonyl@fiskars.demon.co.uk
*and:*
Richard Sankey & Son Ltd.
Bennerly Road
Nottingham NG6 8PE
0115 927 7335
Email: info@rsankey.co.uk
*Wide range of craft equipment.*

**Homecrafts Direct**
Unit 2, Wanlip Road
Syston
Leicester LE7 1PD
Tel: 0116 269 7733
Email: info@homecrafts.co.uk
www.homecrafts.co.uk
*Mail-order service. Selection of handmade*
*papers and range of craft products.*

**Paperchase**
Flagship Store and Main Office
213 Tottenham Court Road
London W1T 7PS
Tel: 020 7467 6200
Mail order tel: 0161 839 1500
Email: mailorder@paperchase.co.uk
www.paperchase.co.uk
*Retailers of stationery, wrapping paper and art*
*materials. Call for your nearest outlet.*

**T N Lawrence**
208 Portland Road
Hove
East Sussex BN3 5QT
Tel: 01273 260 260
www.lawrence.co.uk
*Carries a large range of papers as well as*
*general artist's materials.*

**The Stencil Store**
41a Heronsgate Road
Chorleywood
Hertfordshire WD3 5BL
Tel: 01923 285 577
Email: stencilstore@onetel.com
www.stencilstore.com
*Supply wide range of stencil designs. Phone for*
*nearest store or to order catalogue.*

**Viking Industrial Products Ltd.**
Unit 1, Coronation Business Park
Hardings Road, Keighley
West Yorkshire BD21 3ND
Tel: 01535 610 373
Email: sales@vikingtapes.co.uk
www.vikingtapes.co.uk
*Huge range of tapes and adhesives.*

**VV Rouleaux**
6 Marylebone High Street
London W1M 3PB
Tel: 020 7224 5179
Fax: 020 7224 5193
Email: marylebone@vvrouleaux.com
www.vvrouleaux.com
*Huge selection of ribbons, trimmings,*
*feathers, fabric and paper flowers.*

## Australia

**Artwise Amazing Paper**
186 Enmore Road
Enmore
NSW 2042
Tel: 02 9519 8237
www.amazingpaper.com.au

**Lincraft**
www.lincraft.com.au
*General craft supplier. Stores throughout Australia.*

**Myer Centre, Rundle Mall**
Adelaide, SA 5000
Tel: 02 8231 6611

**Myer Centre, Queen Street**
Brisbane, QLD 4000
Tel: 07 3221 0064

**Shop D02/D03**
Canberra Centre
Bunda Street
Canberra, ACT 2601
Tel: 02 6257 4516

**Australia on Collins**
Melbourne, VIC 3000
Tel: 03 9650 1609

**Imperial Arcade, Pitt Street**
Sydney, NSW 2000
Tel: 02 9221 5111

**Paper Fantasy**
256a Charters Towers Road
Hermit Park, QLD 4812
Tel: 07 4725 1272

**Paperwright**
124 Lygon Street
Carlton, VIC 3053
Tel: 03 9663 8747

**Spotlight**
Tel: 1800 656 256
www.spotlight.com.au
*General craft supplier. Call for nearest store.*

## South Africa

**Art Shop**
140a Victoria Avenue
Benoni West 1503
Tel/Fax: 011 421 1030

**Arts, Crafts and Hobbies**
72 Hibernia Street
George 6529
Tel/Fax: 044 874 1337
*Mail-order service available.*

**Pen and Art**
Shop 313, Musgrave Centre
Musgrave Road
Durban 4001
Tel/Fax: 031 201 0094

**Bowker Arts and Crafts**
52 4th Avenue
Newton Park
Port Elizabeth 6001
Tel: 041 365 2487
Fax: 041 365 5306

**Centurion Kuns**
Shop 45, Eldoraigne Shopping Mall
Saxby Road
Eldoraigne 0157
Tel/Fax: 012 654 0449

**Crafty Supplies**
Shop UG 2, Stadium on Main
Main Road, Claremont 7700
Cape Town
Tel: 021 671 0286
Fax: 021 671 0308

**Creative Papercraft**
64 Judd Street
Horizon1724
Tel/Fax: 011 763 5682

**L & P Stationery and Art**
141 Zastron Street
Westdene
Bloemfontein 9301
Tel: 051 430 1085
Fax: 051 430 4102

**Le Papier du Port**
Gardens Centre
Cape Town 8000
Tel: 021 462 4796
Fax: 021 461 9281
*Mail-order service available.*

## New Zealand

**Brush & Palette**
50 Lichfield Street
Christchurch
Tel/Fax: 03 366 3088

**Fine Art Papers**
200 Madras Street
Christchurch
Tel: 03 379 4410
Fax: 03 379 4443

**Gordon Harris Art Supplies**
4 Gillies Avenue
Newmarket, Auckland
Tel: 09 520 4466
Fax: 09 520 0880
*and:*
31 Symonds Street
Auckland Central
Tel: 09 377 9992

**Littlejohns**
170 Victoria Street
Wellington
Tel: 04 385 2099
Fax: 04 385 2090

**Studio Art Supplies**
81 Parnell Rise
Parnell, Auckland
Tel: 09 377 0302
Fax: 09 377 7657

**G Webster & Co Ltd.**
44 Manners Street
Wellington
Tel: 04 384 2134
Fax: 04 384 2968

# INDEX